DINOSAURS
OF THE PREHISTORIC ERA

MODERN PUBLISHING
A DIVISION OF UNISYSTEMS, INC.
NEW YORK, NEW YORK 10022

CONTENTS

ANATOSAURUS
(ah-NAT-uh-sawr-us)

Anatosaurus belonged to a family of dinosaurs called **Hadrosaurs**. They had jaws that were shaped like a duck's beak. They were also called **duck-billed** dinosaurs. Anatosaurus was one of the last **species** of dinosaur to become extinct.

Anatosaurus had a smooth, round head. It had strong back legs and could run very fast. This **herbivore** ate plants, leaves, and small shrubs. One set of Anatosaurus remains was even found with pine needles in its stomach!

Some Anatosaurus remains have been found with pieces of skin preserved. This is a very unusual find. Its skin had a pebbly texture, like the skin of a modern-day lizard.

Anatosaurus had over 1,000 tiny teeth in its mouth which it used to munch on vegetation.

4

DEINONYCHUS
(dyne-ON-ik-us)

Deinonychus was one of the deadliest hunters that ever lived. Its name means "terrible claw." It got its name because of a curved toe with a claw that it had on each foot. The claw was used to catch and kill its prey.

Deinonychus was a very fast runner. It ran on its other three toes, lifting the curved claw as it ran. Balancing on one leg, this **carnivore** would use its sharp claw to rip the bodies of other dinosaurs. Deinonychus had very strong thigh muscles. This made its legs and claws dangerous weapons.

Deinonychus used its tail for balance when running and attacking. It had a large head, good eyesight, and sharp teeth.

Deinonychus weighed only about as much as a full-grown man, but stood 11 feet tall.

6

PACHYCEPHALOSAURUS
(pak-ee-SEF-uh-lo-sawr-us)

Pachycephalosaurus was a member of a family of dinosaurs known as **bonehead** dinosaurs. They got this name because all members of this family had very thick skulls.

Some boneheads were less than three feet long. Pachycephalosaurus was one of the biggest members of the family, measuring 15 feet in length and weighing 450 pounds.

It used its very thick skull to charge at its enemies and knock them senseless. Its skull was 10 inches of thick bone, so it packed quite a wallop. Pachycephalosaurus also had some small, bony spikes jutting up from its nose and sharp knobs around the back of its head. It may have also used its ramming head to fight for territory with others of its species.

Pachycephalosaurus had a thick skull, but it also had a very tiny brain.

PSITTACOSAURUS
(SIT-uh-ko-sawr-us)

Psittacosaurus was considered a member of the **Ceratopsian** family—a family of horned dinosaurs. That was odd, because Psittacosaurus had no horns. But it had a deep, mouth that looked like the beak of a parrot.

This small herbivore had relatively few teeth. It used its sharp beak to rip leaves off trees. Its eyes and nostrils were set high on the sides of its head.

Psittacosaurus had four toes on each foot. One of its toes was a stump, like a short thumb. It had four fingers on each hand and had claws on each finger and toe. Psittacosaurus walked on all four limbs and stood up on its back legs to reach plants and branches.

Even the biggest Psittacosaurus was only five feet tall—the size of a small person.

RUTIODON
(ROO-tee-o-don)

Rutiodon belongs to a family of dinosaurs called **Crocodilians**. They were called this because they resemble the modern-day crocodile. This **amphibian** had a long skull and body. Its body measured 12 feet in length. Bony plates called **scutes** covered its back and tail. These served as armor against attackers.

Its nostrils were set far back on its head and were raised above its skull on two bumps. These high nostrils allowed Rutiodon to breathe while it waited underwater for its prey.

This powerful meat-eater lived in lakes and streams, and preyed on small dinosaurs. When it couldn't eat the meat of other dinosaurs, Rutiodon settled for fish.

Rutiodon had strong maternal instincts, and would fiercely protect its nest of eggs from predators.

12

SCOLOSAURUS
(SKO-luh-sawr-us)

This plant-eater was a member of the **Ankylosaur** family of dinosaurs. Scolosaurus was 17 feet long. Its body was covered with armor-like plates and sharp, horned spikes. Its short tail had a club on the end. On this club were two long spikes.

The spiked club made an excellent weapon. With a powerful swing of the tail, Scolosaurus could break the neck or the leg of the huge, meat-eating dinosaurs that would attack it.

Scolosaurus was a peaceful dinosaur who would only fight in self-defense. It usually lived in rocky caves. Its natural color helped to **camouflage** it, when it could not get to the shelter of a cave.

When attacked, Scolosaurus would lie on its belly, using its armor-plated back for protection.

14

SPINOSAURUS
(SPY-nuh-sawr-us)

Spinosaurus had a large spine covered with skin on its back. This gave it the appearance of having a sail on its back. Spinosaurus was a large dinosaur, growing to a size of 40 feet and weighing seven tons. The spines on its back were six feet high.

Its sails served several purposes. Rival males may have shown off their sails to threaten each other. The sails were also used for heat exchange. In the morning, when Spinosaurus was cold, it would turn its sail towards the sun, bringing heat to its body. This would give it a better chance to catch cold-blooded prey that had not yet warmed up. In the heat of midday, Spinosaurus would turn away from the sun, allowing heat to leave its body through the sail.

Paleontologists *knew that Spinosaurus was a meat-eater because it had teeth that were* **serrated** *like a steak knife.*

16

TYRANNOSAURUS REX
(tye-RAN-uh-sawr-us rex)

Tyrannosaurus Rex was a giant, meat-eating killer. It was 40 feet long from head to tail, and 18 feet tall. Its legs were like large pillars.

Even though it was huge, Tyrannosaurus Rex could run at a speed of nearly 20 miles per hour. But it could only maintain this speed for a short time. Paleontologists believe that it hunted by first hiding. When its victim came along, Tyrannosaurus Rex would only have a short chase to catch its next meal.

It would crash into its prey with its enormous head. This would stun the victim. Tyrannosaurus Rex would then finish the kill with a bone-crushing bite from its gigantic mouth. Its razor-sharp teeth were six inches long.

Even though it had to kill its food most of the time, Tyrannosaurus Rex probably preferred to eat carrion.

PTERANODON
(tar-AN-o-don)

Pteranodon means "winged and toothless." This leathery-winged, fish-eating creature was not really a dinosaur. It was part of the group of flying reptiles known as **Pterosaurs**.

Pteranodon glided through the air on wind currents, searching prehistoric waters for its next meal. When it spotted a fish, it would dive to the surface of the water and pluck the fish out with its sharp, pointy beak.

The Pteranodon's **crest** was six feet long—more than twice the size of its head. This crest started at the tip of its toothless beak and ran way past the back of its head. A big crest was not present in every Pteranodon fossil found. Only some of these flying reptiles had it.

Pteranodon weighed only 33 pounds and had a body about the size of a turkey.

DIPLODOCUS
(dih-PLOD-uh-kus)

Diplodocus was one of the largest of the **Sauropods**. It could grow to 91 feet in length, with a 26-foot-long neck, and a 45-foot-long tail. Its head was quite small, and it had two rows of peg-like teeth.

Its teeth shredded leaves as they were pulled from tree branches. With its long neck, Diplodocus could see over tall trees. It could spot enemies approaching from far away, which was a good thing. Diplodocus was a slow-moving herbivore and was not able to outrun meat-eaters.

Its tail was so big that it often dragged on the ground as Diplodocus walked.

Even though Diplodocus was 91 feet long, it weighed only 11 tons.

22

GLOSSARY

Amphibian—An animal that lives both on land and in the water.

Ankylosaur—An armor-plated family of dinosaurs.

Boneheads—A family of dinosaurs with very thick skulls.

Camouflage—To disguise or blend in.

Carnivore—Meat-eating animal.

Carrion—The meat of an animal that is already dead. A dinosaur that eats carrion is eating the meat from an animal it did not kill.

Ceratopsian—A group of plant-eating dinosaurs that had horns or frills on their heads.

Crest—A crown-like piece of bone that stuck out of the back of the head of some dinosaurs.

Crocodilian—A family of prehistoric amphibious reptiles that greatly resembled modern-day crocodiles.

Duck-billed—A family of dinosaurs that had long, flat bills, like those of a duck.

Hadrosaurs—Duck-billed dinosaurs.

Herbivore—A plant-eating animal.

Paleontologist—A scientist who studies dinosaurs.

Predators—Hunters.

Pterosaurs—Flying reptiles that lived at the same time as the dinosaurs.

Sauropods—Four-legged, plant-eating dinosaurs. These gentle giants were the biggest of all the dinosaurs.

Scutes—Bony plates found on the back of Crocodilians.

Serrated—Jagged edged.

Species—A family of animals.